Black Belt Excellence

9 SECRETS

Reveal the TRUTH About Family Martial Arts Training

"A Family That Kicks Together, Sticks Together!"

by Master Phil Nguyen

7th Degree Black Belt in ITF Taekwon-Do
1st Degree Black Belt in Kanzenbudo Jiu-Jitsu

Black Belt Excellence Inc.
http://blackbeltexcellencebook.com

Copyright Page

Black Belt Excellence: 9 Secrets Reveal the Truth About Family Martial Arts Training

ISBN 978-0-9936444-1-2

Copyright © 2014 Black Belt Excellence Inc.

Published by Black Belt Excellence Inc. (http://blackbeltexcellencebook.com)

Contact: inquiry@blackbeltexcellencebook.com

These rules have been established to protect the rights and ownership of Black Belt Excellence Inc., and to ensure that this work is upheld as its own.

Table of Contents

Introduction

The Challenge

Do you face any of these challenges?

- You dread the idea of your child being bullied.
- You wish you could find a way to channel your child's boundless energy.
- Your son or daughter lacks self-confidence or self-esteem.
- Your teenager needs more focus and discipline to succeed in school and in life.
- You wish you could stop your busy life from destroying your health and your family life.

If you answered yes to any of the above questions, then keep reading, because family martial arts training can help you improve your current circumstance.

1

My Promise

My promise is to share my unique perspective as a professional martial artist who has been training, teaching, competing, and coaching thousands of students over the past 30 years helping them discover their best selves, and hopefully to inspire and to instruct you on how you can do the same through family martial arts training.

Therefore, I have the following objectives for this book: (1) to persuade you to enroll your child/children in a martial arts program; (2) to persuade you to enroll in a martial arts program alongside your child/children; and (3) to dispel the myth that martial arts is about violence but rather that family martial arts training is about virtues.

Martial arts is more than kicking and punching. It is an art, a sport, a philosophy, and a way of life. From a family perspective, I believe it can help you live the life of your dreams. Why do I make this bold assertion? From my experience, when kids are more focused, more respectful, and more disciplined at home and school, then parents are very happy. When kids are participating in healthy activity for their mind and body and are happy doing something they love, then parents are very happy. When kids are working hard to achieve their goals on their way to becoming contributing members of society, then parents are very happy. And when parents join in all the fun and fitness with the rest of their family members, well then, I believe you are truly living the dream, as a family.

When your kids find something they love doing, they'll eventually gain more competence, and along with it will increase their confidence in being able to achieve anything they want in life. And when that happens, as a parent you are in fact living the life of your dreams. You and your kids go to bed at night with a smile on your face, peacefulness in your mind, and love in your heart. Family martial arts training can help you.

The Results

I recommend sending children to a good martial arts school to increase their focus, to get them to concentrate better, and to gain more self-control – world-renowned child psychologist Dr.

Ruth Peters (featured on *The Oprah Winfrey Show,
Good Morning America, CBS Good Morning,*
NBC's *Today, CNN Morning News,* and *MSNBC*)

Much like the millions of martial arts practitioners around the world, you too can benefit from the life-enhancing qualities of family martial arts training.

In my own experience as co-owner, along with my wife Amelia Nguyen, of the award-winning Black Belt Excellence Martial Arts Academy located in Canada's Capital of Ottawa, Ontario, we have witnessed transformative results:

- Shy kids become super-CONFIDENT.
- HYPER kids gain CONTROL of their energy and emotions.
- Girls with low SELF-ESTEEM turn into SELF-ASSURED young women.
- Boys with low SELF-CONFIDENCE turn into SUCCESSFUL young men.
- STRESSED-Out moms transform into SENSATIONALLY POWERFUL women.

- OUT-OF-SHAPE dads get into the BEST SHAPE of their lives.
- A student with DOWN Syndrome who UP-lifts our spirits.
- Students from SINGLE-parent homes Who DOUBLE up their efforts in class.
- ORDINARY people accomplish EXTRAORDINARY things they never thought possible themselves.

You see, Black Belt Excellence is a metaphor for you achieving personal excellence at home, school, work, and your community.

Are you looking for more evidence, results, and success stories of the life-enhancing qualities of martial arts?

Ask your neighbor how martial arts has impacted their kid.

Ask your doctor or child psychologist what they think about the benefits of training in martial arts for mind and body. (I know because many of my students come to me referred by doctors.)

Go to your neighborhood martial arts school and don't just ask the instructor; ask the parents waiting around the reception area. Better yet, ask the parents walking out of the dojo (training area) how they're enjoying their martial arts experience.

From my experience, when I ask people about the impact martial arts has had on them, there's usually an immediate change in their physiology as they become more animated and radiate more energy as they recount the multiple positive benefits of how they and/or their child has improved dramatically.

The Obstacles

Still not convinced? Let's look at three obstacles that would prevent you from training in the martial arts and how you can overcome them.

1. Time

You have a busy life and a busy schedule and you juggle multiple roles and goals. But think of the consequences of keeping up a weekly routine of work and family life and no physical activity. I challenge you to make the time for your children, to make the time for your family, to make the time for your sanity, to make the time for your health, and to make the time for yourself.

I can assure you that the one or two hours per week you invest will be time well spent. I truly believe that martial arts will be the highlight of your day and a path to a more empowered life.

2. Energy

After a long day at work, home, or running your business, you're probably stressed, exhausted, and ready to crash in front of the TV with a bag of potato chips. Don't do it. Avoid getting into a negative cycle which will only keep you and your family from discovering and becoming your best self.

Perhaps you already have your kids in other activities and spend the week chauffeuring them around and you use their class time to socialize with other parents, or simply use it as down time to take a nap or check your e-mails on your smart phone.

What about yourself? If your kids are out there being active and staying fit, do you think there could be a more constructive way for you to spend your time and do the same? When you get on the mat and train with your kids, you will surely get a surge of endorphins which will boost your energy. You may feel physically tired but you will feel mentally sharp and spiritually fulfilled, and you will get a great night's sleep.

3. Money

With all your basic expenses, groceries, and family vacations, you may think that paying tuition to train in the martial arts is a luxury. Here's an interesting quiz for you. When you need to buy school supplies for your kids, where do you go? The local office supply or school supply store. When you need to buy food for your family, where do you go? The grocery store or farmer's market.

But when you want your kids to gain more self-confidence, focus, and discipline, where do you go? A martial arts school. And aren't these life skills priceless? They are, by definition, skills that will last for a lifetime. And remember that it's not only kids who could benefit from life skills. Do you think you could further develop your own self-confidence, focus, and discipline? If you value these life skills, then your martial arts training tuition is not so much an expense as it is an investment.

In any case, most modern martial arts schools offer low-cost introductory fees so you can at least try it to see if it's for you. You can also ask for family discounts. And of course, you can always try a city-run program, which is very affordable, at least to get you started.

Student Success Stories

Annuj perceives his martial arts instructor as a positive influence in his life. He thoroughly enjoys going to the classes. We make reference to the 8 Life Skills to influence good behavior. Sometimes we ask our son, "Would your teacher like this unacceptable behavior?" (based on a particular life skill). And we have seen him change to a positive behavior immediately. – Ramani K. and Kamal K.

9

Our son has shown an improvement in physical strength and in his self-esteem, which we feel helped him succeed in his swimming. – Stephen and Cindy L.

Since last month, we have noticed tremendous changes in our son Kevin's behavior. He is always answering our requests properly; and for any help we provide to him, he always shows his appreciation. Considering he just started training last November, we are really impressed and thank you all for your efforts. – Li G. and Yuan X.

On the weekend, we brought the children to the park. I was pitching a baseball to Emily's older brother and Emily was ready to retrieve it. When Tommy made a great, hard hit, I was impressed, until I saw it coming fast and hard, directly at Emily's head. Her reaction time was amazing. She dropped to the ground and the ball sailed over her. She laughed and said, "Hey, that was just like at Taekwon-Do!" (Referring to when the instructors swing the bats over the children's heads and they must...) – Patti C.

About Master Phil

My Story of Struggle is ...

When I was a teenager, I had a lot of anger. I argued with my mom, defied my dad, yelled, and broke things. Perhaps it was teenage angst and a surge in testosterone, combined with dealing with my parents' divorce at the time. One day, my mom couldn't take it anymore and kicked me out of the house. I went to live with my dad and my step-family in their basement.

It was a very difficult and confusing time in my life.

But then one day, my dad signed me and my step-brother up for a Taekwon-Do class.

Back in the mid-80s, there weren't too many dojangs around (Korean term for martial arts school), let alone teenage kids my age who were training. In fact, I remember being the youngest student in my class. My training took place in the basement garage of a building and I distinctly

11

remember my instructor having me perform my stances up and down the cold concrete floor for most of the class.

This spartan training atmosphere and doing my discipline drills were the beginning of the journey for me as a white belt.

I eventually became accustomed to my routine and would look forward to my Taekwon-Do training days.

As a high school student, I would get up in the morning, pack my school stuff in my backpack, my soccer equipment in my gear bag in my left hand, and my Taekwon-Do dobok (uniform) and sparring equipment in my right hand, and rush to catch the bus to school. And then right after school I would play my soccer game. And then right after my soccer game, I would take the bus to my Taekwon-Do class. Then after a long day, I would go home and do my homework. And then, repeat cycle.

Along this journey of Black Belt Excellence,

- I learned about focus (focusing on my academic and athletic priorities).

- I learned about discipline (managing my schoolwork, my soccer, and my martial arts training).

- I learned about respect. (Once I realized that in martial arts it all begins and ends with respect, I started showing more respect to myself and to my parents. In fact, the first time I bowed to my dad, he almost fainted.)

- I learned about humility. (By unleashing my pent-up anger and aggression on the punching bags, I was able to channel my energy more constructively, and came to realize the error of my ways, apologized to my mom, and eventually returned to live with her and my brother David.)

- I learned about self-control. (Through the discipline of training, I learned to control my emotions, thoughts, and actions and therefore get control in my life and gain more peacefulness in my heart; and I eventually stopped arguing, defying, and yelling at my parents.)

You see, I truly believe that martial arts saved my life.

Martial arts helped me to redefine myself and my relationship with life.

Martial arts shaped the course of my destiny.

Martial arts gave me the confidence to succeed.

My Story of Success is …

Since that humble beginning as a zit-faced, angry and insecure, teenaged, white belt student, I've been on a rather incredible journey and achieved things I would have never imagined.

- Martial arts-wise, I achieved my 7th Degree Black Belt International Master Instructor in ITF Taekwon-Do and recently achieved my 1st Degree Black Belt in Jiu-Jitsu.

- Career-wise, I went on to achieve a Bachelor's Degree in Engineering and Management and became a Certified Master Trainer, a Certified Professional Facilitator, and a Distinguished Toastmaster.

- Business-wise, I co-founded the award-winning Black Belt Excellence Martial Arts Academy in 1988, the first-established and longest-running martial arts school in my city of Kanata.

- Community-wise, I co-created an award-winning Bully Busters program, a free service I offer to local schools teaching children assertiveness skills to deal with conflict in a peaceful and confident manner. I've also helped raise tens of thousands of dollars for my local children's hospital, women's shelter, and mental health hospital. In fact, a room was named after my martial arts academy.

- Family-wise, I'm happily married to Amelia Nguyen and proud father of 2 ninjas, Justice and Jackson.

- Author-wise, I'm now declaring myself as a writer with this book as my first published work and I am currently writing more books in this Black Belt Excellence Series (*9 Secrets to Becoming a Bully Buster* and *9 Secrets to Greater Focus Through Martial Arts Training*) as well as a book on Black Belt Leadership – *9-Point Path to Wisdom, Inspiration, and Enlightenment.*

The MYTH about Martial Arts

So by now you are probably very interested in beginning your martial arts journey, but you may have some apprehensions due to the biggest myth about martial arts.

Some people think that martial arts is about violence when, in fact, family martial arts training is really about virtues.

Some people have this idea that martial arts is all physical; but you will discover that martial arts training also develops your mental and spiritual dimensions. Yes, there is definitely a physical aspect to the training and you will surely get a great workout as you develop your endurance, flexibility, power, speed, strength, balance, and coordination. But as you do so, you will also empower your mind through the various repetitions of techniques towards mastery which will improve your focus, self-discipline, and self-confidence. Eventually, as you progress on your journey of self-discovery, you will have a greater spirit and positive energy about you as you reveal your inner power, courage, and maximum potential.

Some people have preconceived notions that martial arts will make their child more physical and aggressive, when the fact of the matter is that martial arts will make him or her gain more impulse control and self-regulation. Martial arts training helps children with impulsivity (which is the failure to resist a temptation, urge or impulse that may harm oneself or others) by providing a physical outlet through which students can unleash their pent up energy (positive or negative) in a safe and controlled environment while teaching patience through the mastering of the art and delayed gratification working towards their next belt level of proficiency. Martial arts training helps students with self-regulation (which is the ability to respond appropriately to the pressures of life and every day situations) by following our code of ethics, the positive support group of fellow students, and the disciplined environment that is expected in a martial arts school.

Some people feel that martial arts will scare their shy and introverted child; but the good news is that martial arts will actually boost his or her self-confidence and self-esteem.

Some people believe that martial arts is about kicking and punching; but the real truth of the matter is that it is about the perfection of character based on a moral code of ethics. For example, in ITF Taekwon-Do, students recite the Student Oath at the beginning of every class:

I shall observe the tenets of Taekwon-Do (Courtesy, Integrity, Perseverance, Self-Control, Indomitable Spirit).

I shall respect the instructor and seniors.

I shall never misuse Taekwon-Do.

I shall be a champion of freedom and justice.

I shall build a more peaceful world.

The samurai had a code of ethics known as "The Seven Virtues of Bushido: Morality, Courage, Benevolence, Respect, Honesty, Honor, and Loyalty."

Some people assume that what they see in the movies is martial arts; but the reality is, it is the ultimate personal development program that develops your mind, body and spirit. Yes, martial arts action in the movies can be spectacular and fun to watch, but that only represents one aspect of the vast field of martial arts. Martial arts as a whole can include study of self-defense, anatomy, physiology, motivation, fitness, exercise, etiquette, tradition, history, geography, life skills, enlightenment, art, philosophy, sport, and a way of life.

Some people perceive that martial arts is about hurting people. However, you would be surprised to know that family martial arts training is about building a more peaceful world. When you train in the martial arts, you learn how to hurt people to defend yourself and your loved ones. Paradoxically, once you learn how to hurt, and you understand the peaceful philosophy of martial arts as a means of self-defense and self-protection, you will most likely choose to not hurt others, either physically or emotionally, including your own family members and loved ones. You realize the fragility of human life and the preciousness of the human condition, which makes you more compassionate, gentle, and peaceful.

I hope you now understand that martial arts is not about violence, but rather that it is about virtues.

The NEW SOLUTION/FRAMEWORK that I will teach is ... 9 Secrets Reveal the Truth About Family Martial Arts Training.

Secret #1: The 5 Unfair Advantages that Martial Arts Offers Compared to Other Activities

What is the unique edge that martial arts offers compared to other sports and activities?

Unfair Advantage #1 – Martial arts not only enhances your life, it could save your life.

First of all, please note that I love sports and doing various physical activities as I've played many sports in my life and continue to be actively involved in sports for myself and my children.

However, martial arts is much more than a physical activity.

Martial arts is a combination of art, sport, philosophy, and a way of life; and it totally enhances your life.

Martial arts is art as it is a form of self-expression where you can express yourself through your deeds and your character.

Martial arts is sport as you get physical exercise, you can choose to compete in tournaments, and you get a great workout.

Martial arts is a philosophy based on values such as courtesy, integrity, perseverance, self-control, and indomitable spirit that promotes the building of a more peaceful world.

Martial arts is a way of life that helps you develop a strong mind, body, and spirit, so that you can be the best you can be and make a difference in the world around you.

It is said that everyone should learn the 2 S's: swimming and self-defense. Why? Because both of them could save your life. So martial arts not only enhances your life, it could save it as well.

Self-defense is definitely one of the most valuable things I have learned, for through the practice of self-defense I have also learned to exercise self-control and greatly improve my self-confidence. – Tyler D.

Unfair Advantage #2 – In martial arts, no one gets benched.

When I play a soccer game, I'll be on the field for only a portion of the time, substituting with other players.

When I watch a hockey game, I'll see my favorite players on the ice for only a portion of the time, and sometimes even benched by the coach for whatever reason.

But when you train in the martial arts, you are smiling, sweating, and learning 100% of the time.

You see, in martial arts, no one gets benched.

In martial arts, no one gets left behind.

In martial arts, there are no scoreboards or statistics, but there is character development.

In martial arts, there are no comparisons against others, just comparison against your former self.

In martial arts, although there is competition, the real competition is against your own self.

In martial arts, no one gets benched and everyone gets to participate.

Student Success Story

Gifted kids are very fast learners, if they are interested (big if here). They grasp big topics easily, have excellent memories and are avid readers. When they get interested in a topic, they get very interested. And if not, well then good luck to the parent or teacher trying to teach and motivate! These kids are passionate about their own interests!

Often the regular classroom can't contain gifted kids. They want to learn more, go into more depth and learn more quickly than their peers. Often they are forced to wait for others to catch up. And sometimes their own passionate interests are not followed up in as much detail as they would like. It seems to them that their interests are downplayed in favor of doing endless worksheets and drills. In school, gifted kids run the risk of not being challenged and not being engaged all the time.

Well martial arts training helped our son because in martial arts "No one gets benched." Every student can develop at his own pace. Gifted kids are always engaged when training in martial arts. Everyone is learning, all the time. No one is forced to wait for others to catch up. Martial arts keeps gifted minds engaged! – Joan B.

Unfair Advantage #3 – Martial Arts leverages the Triangle of Success.

People often try to find balance in their lives.

Kids try to balance home life with school life.

Parents try to balance home life with work life.

But when you try to balance two elements, focusing on one leads to focusing less on the other, weighing more in the favor of one over the other.

But when you add a third element, you start a triangulation process, which is very powerful. That third element makes all the difference in creating what is called the Triangle of Success.

For kids, the Triangle of Success is balancing home, school, and martial arts.

For parents, the Triangle of Success is balancing home, work, and martial arts.

And therein lies the magic. The third element of martial arts training serves as a great motivator and accountability tool for you and your kids.

When you as a parent tell your kids to do something, they might listen.

When the teachers at school tell your kids to do something, they might listen.

But when the martial arts instructor who serves as a third party reinforces everything the parents and teachers say and tells your kids to do something, they do listen.

Why? Because most people simply try to balance school/work and home life, with little extra motivation to drive them forward. But for kids, since they love the action, coolness, and belt promotion system of the martial arts, they feel more accountable to listen to their "sensei" who is simply reinforcing what you and their school teachers are trying to teach them. Also kids also tend to respect the uniform and look up to Black Belts as a role model in their lives. And so they end up behaving better at home and performing better at school.

"Children go where there is excitement, but they stay where there is love."

Because of the excitement of martial arts, the kids look forward to going to class, and do something they love that keeps them active. But what keeps them there is the loving, positive, and encouraging environment that martial arts provide.

And this is how you can leverage the martial arts Triangle of Success to raise confident, respectful, and disciplined kids.

Student Success Story

The benefit I have gained through my martial arts training is that in my early grades in school I had struggled, but I've since gotten better as I've advanced through my grades. – Dylan M., age 12

Unfair Advantage #4 – Martial arts is the ultimate personal development program.

Martial arts is the ultimate personal development program because it helps you develop mind, body, and spirit all at the same time.

If you wanted to empower your mind, you could read a book, go to a seminar, or attend a course.

If you wanted to energize your body, you could go for a job, do a yoga class, or play a team sport with your friends.

If you wanted to enlighten your spirit, you could say a prayer, meditate peacefully, or go to your place of worship.

But when you train in the martial arts, you develop your mind, body, and spirit all at the same time. You develop your mind through learning about martial arts techniques, philosophy, and yourself; you exercise your body through the sweat-inducing physical exercises, dynamic drills and skills, and self-defense training; and you engage your spirit through meditation exercises and a lot of laughter.

When it comes to mind, body, and spirit, most of us are cultivating only one or two of these three factors at any given time, which means you are not living up to your full potential.

For example, if you have a strong mind and a strong body but not a strong spirit, you will lack that drive and dedication to get up in the morning to live the life of your dreams.

If you have a strong mind and spirit, but you are not taking care of your body, then you will surely fall prey to illness or have poor health and lack the motivation to take action.

If you have a strong body and a strong spirit, but you are lacking a sharp mind, you will lack the clarity, focus, and discipline to achieve your goals and realize your dreams.

When you train in the martial arts it is one of those rare activities where you can enhance and strengthen your mind, your body, and your spirit. And when you engage all three elements, it becomes a performance multiplier. When all three are in full effect I believe that you can discover your best self and achieve awesomeness in your life, in your home, in your work, and in the community.

In turn this makes you a better person. When you become a better person you attract positive people in your life and better, higher quality opportunities in your life.

This is why I believe that you can live the life of your dreams through martial arts training by developing a strong mind, body, and spirit.

Student Success Stories

Training in the martial arts is a constant challenge for mind, body, and spirit. I need to constantly remind myself of my abilities, and the sentence "I can do it – I will do it" applies to adults in the same manner it applies to kids and beginners. – Lt.-Col. Stefan K.

Much to my dismay as a former amateur baseball player and sports fan, my son Nolan never gravitated toward traditional team sports. As a parent, however, I wanted him to find something he could embrace, that would provide him with the benefits of exercise, camaraderie, teamwork and all those things we're told are valuable as we progress through our youth. Based on my personal experience, I also wanted him to be part of something that would provide a lifetime of memories and friendships.

What I didn't expect, upon enrolling him in the martial arts, was the impact his participation would have on his personality and character. From the moment he first put on his uniform, the expression on his face told me he had found his passion. As he progressed through the first belt levels, I noticed a change in his attitude and his level of respect towards everyone around him.

The family martial arts training environment promotes positivity, while the leadership provides structure, commands respect, and encourages personal growth. The instructors provide a perfect mix of support, encouragement, pressure, criticality, respect, positivity and leadership.

Nolan's transformation over the year and a half he's been part of the program has been eye opening. He's grown from a typical shy, reserved, lazy (yes, he's as guilty as the next one) boy into a motivated, respectful, confident and well-rounded person.

I am proud of the person he is, the man he is becoming, and the friends he has gained through attending classes. I am beyond thrilled that he has found something that provides him with such an outstanding life experience, and am confident he will reach his potential in martial arts and as a person as a result of his participation. – Stephen W.

Unfair Advantage #5 – Martial Arts is the ultimate structured, goal-based activity you can do together as a family.

When you think about family activities such as swimming, skiing, skating, rollerblading, or bicycling, these are great activities but not so much structured but rather for leisure purposes.

When you think about team sports, you know you can't really play on the same football team as your son or jump on the mat and do gymnastics with your daughter.

You can coach or volunteer, but you are not actually participating alongside your kids.

However, martial arts is the ultimate structured, goal-based activity you can do together as a family, so take advantage of this unfair advantage martial arts has over other activities. It is the ultimate activity because it is fun and fitness, but in a disciplined environment. It is structured because there are set class times and certain rules of safety and etiquette everyone must follow under the supervision of a qualified black belt instructor. It is goal-based because each student can strive to ascend from white belt to black belt at his or her own pace or even test through the belts together as a family.

And just like your favorite animated child's movie caters to both the children and their parents for fun and a good time, so too does a martial arts class cater to both the children and their parents for fun and a good time.

What you will find in a family martial arts training class is that it follows the classic Rule of SSL. That is, for every class, the goal is for you to be Smiling, Sweating, and Learning.

Smiling means you'll be having fun, spending quality time with your family, and making friends.

Sweating means you'll be getting a great workout, burning calories, and staying in shape.

Learning means you'll be learning about martial arts, about yourself, and the world around you.

Every time you walk out of the class, you will all walk out a better son, daughter, brother, sister, mother, father, husband, or wife.

Martial Arts class will be the highlight of your day, the path to an empowered life.

Student Success Stories

I started training martial arts when my son Karl was six years old. Like many other parents waiting for their child I thought to myself: "Why am I waiting outside? Why don't I train as well?" And that led to me joining the Academy. I have been training every week since with my whole family and we are all Black Belts. – Mario D., age 46

Martial arts has allowed me to share great experiences with my family which will be the foundation to remain a close family involved in each other's life for years to come. – Chantal M., age 41

Secret #2: The Magic Formula for Harnessing the Boundless Energy of Your 3-5 Year Old

In all my years of teaching thousands of kids and interacting with thousands of parents, I found the following statements to be true:

1. As parents, we all want our kids to be happy and good kids.

2. As parents, we all want our kids to be healthy and safe kids.

3. Kids, on the other hand, want one thing, and one thing only. That is to have fun!

The beautiful thing about martial arts is that it incorporates the Magic Formula for harnessing the boundless energy of your 3-5 year old.

Since we all want our kids to be happy and good kids, kids learn life skills, such as courtesy, respect, focus, discipline, self-control, responsibility, cooperation, and learning.

Since we all want our kids to be healthy and safe, kids learn safety and self-defense skills as well as bullying response and stranger awareness skills.

And since kids want one thing, and one thing only, and that is to have fun, they get to practice cool martial arts skills that get their bodies moving, their minds focusing, and their hearts laughing with joy in a positive and supportive environment.

So the Magic Formula integrates the learning of life skills, safety skills, and martial arts skills to not only harness your child's boundless energy, but it gets them to sleep well at night, which always puts a smile on a parent's face.

Through Martial Arts Training, Your 3-5 Year Old Will:

- Be physically and mentally active.
- Learn polite greetings and manners.
- Learn the importance of self-care.

- Start to understand the concept of listening to parents and teachers.
- Learn to focus more.
- Develop physical balance, flexibility, and coordination.
- Learn to live and play safely.
- Increase awareness of body and space.
- Learn to share and co-operate with others.
- Make friends.

Secret #3: The Biggest Challenge Boys and Girls Aged 6-11 Have and How to Boost Their Odds of Overcoming It

"Our goal is not to prepare the path for the children, but to prepare the children for the path."

In my 30+ years of teaching thousands of school-aged children through the teaching of martial arts, as well as my wife's and my Bully Busters program that we have taught at grade schools, I have observed a common challenge facing boys and girls aged 6-11.

For boys, I have observed and discovered that the biggest challenge they have is lack of self-confidence. I define self-confidence as the belief that one has the ability to succeed.

For girls, I have observed and discovered that the biggest challenge they have is lack of self-esteem. I define self-esteem as the feeling of self-worth one has and that she is deserving of happiness, respect, and success.

Of course, self-confidence and self-esteem, or the lack thereof, are not exclusively gender-based and apply to both boys and girls.

Now, what's interesting is that when parents need school supplies, they go to the office supply and school supply store. When parents need food, they go to the grocery store. But when parents want their child to gain more self-confidence and more self-esteem, they turn to martial arts.

Yes, martial arts is an excellent activity to boost your children's odds of overcoming a lack of self-confidence and self-esteem.

And I can explain why by first sharing with you my job description as a martial arts master, and most martial arts instructors would agree:

1. Accept students as they are.

2. See them as who they could be.

3. Create opportunities for success.

Allow me to elaborate.

1. Accept students as they are.

This means that regardless of a child's physical, mental, psychological, or social limitations, disabilities, or challenges, I accept students as they are, warts and all. If a child has heart and is willing to put in the work and train hard, anything is possible.

Now this does not mean that martial arts training has a 100% success rate with all students; but martial arts training can do great things and make a huge difference in children's lives.

2. See them as who they could be.

This means that regardless of a student's limiting beliefs, I can often see the student's great potential. My job is to help them further develop their strengths and overcome their weaknesses.

3. Create opportunities for success.

As a martial arts instructor, I don't necessarily teach self-confidence and self-esteem. Rather, I create opportunities for success which develop children's self-confidence and self-esteem.

Various examples of how children training in the martial arts can start building confidence include: counting to 10 for certain class exercises; they can demonstrate a technique in front of a class; they can train for and compete at a tournament and maybe even win a medal; they can practice for a public demonstration; they can participate in a community fundraiser; or they can achieve a belt promotion.

Through Martial Arts Training, Your 6-11 Year Old Will:

- Develop a greater sense of self-confidence.
- Develop self-esteem and a sense of self-worth.

- Act more respectfully toward family members, teachers, and others.

- Increase focus and concentration.

- Enhance memory and listening skills.

- Demonstrate more self-control.

- Understand the importance of taking responsibility.

- Learn to share and promote teamwork.

- Make friends and encourage socialization.

There's a saying that goes, "It is easier to build strong children than to repair broken adults."

By enrolling your children in a character-building martial arts program, you are investing in their future as they build the top twin assets they could possibly have in life: the self-confidence to succeed in life and the self-esteem that they are worthy of success.

Student Success Stories

I have improved my self-confidence and my fitness abilities and have conquered my fear of performing in front of others. – Dan-Vy T.

I believe that martial arts training has greatly improved my self-confidence, self-control, humility, and my integrity. It has had a profound effect on my ability to work under stress; homework and other tasks do not seem like an impending doom upon me, but they merely seem like just another task that needs finishing. – Kevin L.

Through martial arts, I have developed perseverance in not giving up on your goals, self-confidence and believing in yourself for success, and time management balancing school, martial arts, and extra-curricular activities. – Chris C.

Secret #4: How You Can Get Your Child to Better Listen, Really Focus, and Pay Attention (even if he/she has ADD/ADHD)

Does your child show any of these symptoms?

- Has trouble staying focused during play or tasks.

- Appears not to listen when spoken to, seems to be daydreaming.

- Can be easily distracted.

- Makes careless mistakes when doing schoolwork or other activities.

- Thinks about other activities while doing activities.

If you answered yes to any of these questions, you and your child are not alone.

Many children have focus issues, whether due to their being diagnosed with ADD/ADHD or simply because of their young age and the era of dramatic distraction in which we live.

Now, if your child would better listen, really focus, and pay attention (even if he/she has ADD/ADHD), that would be living the dream, wouldn't it? Imagine if your child actually listened to you the first time. Imagine if he or she could really focus on the task at hand, whether it's playing a sport or doing homework. Imagine if your child paid attention to what was going on around him or her.

It is possible. Martial arts training can help. Over the years, I've had a number of students referred to my academy by doctors and child psychologists who recommend that parents enroll their children in the martial arts to help with their focus issues.

Although there's a lot of information out there about professional treatment for ADD/ADHD, studies and research, and even medications, I'd like to offer my perspective as a martial arts instructor who has actually helped hundreds of kids, many of them with focus issues, on a weekly basis. Martial arts produces **results**.

Here are three ways the martial arts teaches your child to better listen, focus, and pay attention:

1. Focus Test

When focus is identified as an issue, one of the first things I do after an awesome introductory martial arts class is ask the child to look at me in the eyes, and ask if he or she wants to be accepted at my academy. If he or she is an existing student, I will ask them if they want to achieve the next level of belt promotion. In both cases, it's usually a resounding yes, because the kids are so engaged and usually love the martial arts.

Then, I challenge the child and say he may join my academy or she may be considered for the next belt level if he or she can pass the Focus Test. I ask the child to look at and focus on my right index finger that I place in front of their eyes for at least 10 seconds, while the parents watch beside us. If the child loses focus, he or she must start from the beginning.

Once he or she agrees, I say, "Are you ready? I'm going to count to ten now, so focus." I start counting, with my right index finger up and them focusing on it; 1, 2, 3, 4, 5, 6, 7, 8, 9, 10 ... 11, 12, 13, 14, 15, 16, 17, 18, 19, 20. Nine times out of ten, they will pass the test. Within less than one minute's time of meeting a child and his or her parents, we have already achieved something great. We have proven that the child can indeed focus, with proper motivation, and more importantly made the child believe in himself. Are you getting excited?

2. Bowing

The very first thing we teach your child is the act of bowing. In martial arts, it all begins and ends with respect. So we bow to the flag, we bow to the instructors, and we bow to each other. How do we bow? We put our feet together, hands to the side, and bow slightly (15-45 degree angle depending on the martial art), while looking at one another in the eyes, which denotes self-confidence as well as respect for the other person. Please note that in Asian culture, one would look down to the floor or close your eyes instead of making eye contact, as a symbol of respect and humility.

So as soon as a child sees an instructor upon arriving at the dojo, he would bow. As soon as your child enters the dojo, he would bow to the flag to show respect. As soon as you and your child enter the dojo, you would bow to each other. Bowing, which is a simple 2-second action, acts as a powerful trigger for your child to be present, mindful, and focused.

Which other activity teaches this? The answer: none.

3. The Three Rules of Concentration: Focus Your Eyes, Focus Your Mind, Good Posture

Focus your eyes means looking ahead in one direction. So I get all the students to stand still in attention stance and have them look straight ahead.

Focus your mind means thinking about one thing only, the task ahead. So the students are taught to think about one thing only, the task ahead.

Good posture denotes the importance of proper physiology, and your child's bodily awareness to be present and concentrating. So the students learn to control their bodily actions and stand upright and still, for the moment.

These three Rules of Concentration engage your child with ADD/ADHD both physically and mentally, and that's what helps him or her focus on the task at hand.

And that is golden. When your child starts to better listen to you and his teachers, really focuses on the task at hand, and pays attention to what is going on around her, then you are truly living the life of your dreams as a parent.

Secret #5: The Two Secret Words of Discipline Guaranteed to Put a Smile on Your Face (and Your Kids)

Can you imagine if your children actually listened to you?

What are the Two Magic Words of Discipline that we teach children in the martial arts that is guaranteed to put a smile on your face and your kids?

"Obey Cheerfully."

When I say these words in class, the parents smile and laugh in gleeful agreement, while the children also smile and laugh at the outrageousness.

Obey = We teach children that this means listening to your parents. Our Martial Arts Triangle of Success teaches children to show good behavior at home, do their best at school, and so they can progress in Martial Arts. However, if they do not listen to or obey their parents at home, they cannot progress in Martial Arts. This is a form of leverage to positively reinforce good behavior at home and support the values of respect and discipline you wish to instill in your children.

Cheerfully = We teach children to not only listen to their parents, but they must do so politely, respectfully, and even cheerfully, despite their disagreement.

It looks something like this:

"Honey, time to stop playing and come set the table and have supper!"

Although your child may be disgruntled and tempted to go into a tantrum, she is taught to show her teeth and say, even reluctantly, "Yes Mom, I'd be happy to!"

"Hey son, let's finish up our game. It's time to clean up and do your homework."

Although your child may be bummed by this, he must grin and bear it and is taught to say, "Yes Dad, right away!"

Just imagine your children listening to you this way as they obey cheerfully. This puts a smile on their face and on yours and it's a beautiful thing, which allows your family to live the life of your dreams through martial arts training.

Student Success Story

One of the things I enjoy the most about my martial arts training is the discipline I learn while training hard. The instructors not only teach you but encourage you as you are doing and being the best you can be. I really appreciate the positive and friendly environment that makes you feel open to others and more self-confident. I really appreciate the opportunity of having fun as a great big family that kicks together and that sticks together! – Eric P., age 12

Secret #6: The 5 Proper Protocols that Instantly Transforms Kids into Leaders

Martial arts is all about movement and posture.

There are physical blocks, punches, and strikes.

There are stances, body angles, distances from opponents.

And then there are the 5 Proper Protocols that instantly transform your kids into leaders.

The 5 Proper Protocols combine rules of etiquette, proper posture, and social conduct:

1. Proper posture.
2. Proper eye contact.
3. Proper handshake.
4. Proper greeting.
5. Proper giving and receiving manner.

Proper posture means back straight, shoulders back, and looking straight ahead, because winners

always know where they are going in life. This
builds self-confidence and leadership skills.

Proper eye contact means
looking at people in the eyes
when speaking with them or
listening to them. This
develops respect for others and
confidence in self.

Proper handshake means
shaking hands firmly and
confidently, which shows good
social manners.

Proper greeting means saying, "Hello, it's a
pleasure to meet you." "Hello, it's a pleasure to see
you." In Martial Arts class, it means answering,
"Yes, Sir!" or "Yes, Ma'am!" At home, it means,
"Yes, Mom!" or "Yes, Dad!" This cultivates
courtesy and respect.

Proper giving and receiving manner means
giving and receiving with politeness and grace. In
martial arts, we put our feet together, extend our
right hand out, support it with our left hand, and do
a slight bow, and say "Thank you, Sir," or "Thank

you, Ma'am." This develops courtesy and an attitude of gratitude.

Teaching kids the 5 Proper Protocols really sets them apart from others and builds their foundation for becoming leaders in our society.

Student Success Story

The most valuable thing that I have learned from martial arts is that confidence is so important and that you must believe in yourself to achieve great things. – Ben K.

Secret #7: 3 + 3 Things You Must Teach Your Child Immediately if They Get Bullied

When I was young I was bullied myself, and was a victim of both racial and psychological bullying. I vowed to myself that when I grew up I would make a difference. Now that I am an adult, a black belt, and a parent, I created the Bully Busters Program with my wife, Amelia Nguyen.

We have since been recognized on a local and national level for our contributions to our community and our country, because using this program we have taught thousands of kids assertiveness skills, non-verbal skills, and verbal skills.

I'm now happy to share with you the key points of our Bully Busters Program, the 3 + 3 Things you must teach your child immediately if he or she gets bullied.

Of course, this assumes you and your child has communicated with his or her teacher and principal.

These are tactical, practical things your child can do and say to better prepare to deal with bullying in a peaceful manner.

The 3 non-verbal skills that you can teach your child.

1. Walk with confidence. Keep your back straight, your shoulders back, look straight forward, because winners know where they are going.

2. Appropriate eye contact. This means glancing at the environment around them, not looking down or aggressively into someone's eyes.

3. Assertive stance. This means you stand with a straight posture, your hands extended in the face of conflict or physical threat, not feeling passive nor aggressive, but rather confident and assertive and that you can defend yourself if necessary.

The 3 verbal skills that you can teach your child.

1. In assertive stance, say, "Please, I don't want any trouble."

2. If the situation escalates, teach your child to say, "Back away, you're too close," while moving to the side, not backwards.

3. If your child really feels threatened, teach him or her to say, "Stop," while extending his or her arm out to stop the bully in his or her tracks.

There is a lot of literature, plus websites, and information on bullying, but this is the stuff that resonates with kids because they understand it and can actually apply it in their schoolyard and everyday situations, when no adults are around to intervene.

It promotes self-reliance and empowers the children to respond appropriately to bullying situations now, and in their future.

Student Success Story

Bully Busters is an amazing workshop for students. It combines physical activity with informative discussion and in-depth conversation. The strategies that the students learn are useful both in and out of the school environment. Master Phil commands respect from students and teaches them to respect themselves and those around them. He has an excellent rapport with students and they love that he is able to remember all of their names. He shares personal stories of being bullied when he was a child. – Kanata Academy Staff

Secret #8: Empowered Teens Are the Hope of Humanity

Every now and again, I'll have an exasperated parent come to me and ask, "Can you help me get my teenage son to stop punching holes in walls?"

I can totally relate because my own teenage years were filled with angst, anger, and insecurities.

Do you remember your teenage years? Dealing with peer pressure, the pressure to succeed in school, and the pressure to find your way in the world. Sadly, when teenagers don't have a moral compass or positive support, they end up losing their way in the world.

In fact, I've believe that the "Disempowered Teens Are the Enemy of Society."

Why? Because a disempowered teenager, one with no dream, directive, or destination, becomes lost. Lost in the crowd, lost in the everyday busyness of society, and lost in their own dark thoughts, feeling disconnected from humanity. And so, they become involved in negative or destructive activities such as bullying, cyberbullying, joining gangs, gang violence, swarming other teenagers, raping other teenagers, teenage pregnancies, dealing drugs, getting addicted to drugs, auto theft, and teenage suicide, to name a few.

Conversely, I believe that "Empowered Teens Are the Hope of Humanity."

When teenagers are given an opportunity to do something that keeps them challenged and engaged, that can keep them around positive role models and a positive peer group, and can channel their aggressive energy towards something more constructive, they become empowered. And when teens are empowered, they become the hope of humanity.

From my experience, I've seen teenagers training in the martial arts achieve great things, for themselves, for their families, and for their community.

- Disempowered teens do drugs, empowered teens do good.
- Disempowered teens are hurt and so hurt others, empowered teens heal and then help others.
- Disempowered teens consume alcohol, empowered teens consume knowledge.
- Disempowered teens lose control of their lives, empowered teens have great plans for their lives.
- Disempowered teens feel the need to prove themselves, empowered teens are focused on improving themselves.
- Disempowered teens practice safe sex, empowered teens practice their katas and patterns.
- Disempowered teens punch holes through walls, empowered teens punch bags and shields in the dojo.
- Disempowered teens destroy people's properties, empowered teens build their character.

- Disempowered teens feel hopeless in our society, empowered teens are the hope of humanity.

I know this to be true, because I've been there and gone from the dark side to the enlightened path. I've witnessed these results and transformations with my own eyes of the thousands of students over the years. My most sincere wish is that if your teen is having problems at school, at home, or in society in general, martial arts training can be a good path for him.

Student Success Stories

I can truly say that my kids and I are better people for training in the martial arts, which have given my son who is now 15, and my daughter who is now 17, a community within our community to grow strong in mind, body and spirit.

Martial arts has cemented a strong foundation and created a positive learning environment based on courtesy, integrity, perseverance, self-control and indomitable spirit. I have seen my children grow in confidence, leadership, physicality and in

65

spirit. Recently, we all achieved our black belts and just saying that gives me a great sense of accomplishment and pride for myself and my teenagers. The teenage years can be a parenting challenge at times, but martial arts creates a scaffold of values which reinforce positive family values at home. Training in martial arts as a family has given me, as a parent, invaluable connections with my teenagers. – Whynn B.

Martial arts have helped me in many ways; from personal fitness, to self-confidence and my leadership abilities. I not only benefit from the actual training but also from the life skills such as discipline and respect. – Ziyad Z., age 15

I strongly believe that martial arts has helped in my spiritual and personal growth. I believe in myself, respect others, and truly believe in building a peaceful community. – Supreena S., age 12

I have thought about quitting before, when training became physically demanding, but what has kept me going is the thought of actually not having martial arts in my life. It has become such a huge part of my life that I can't imagine myself without it. – Michael B.

Secret #9: A Family that Kicks Together, Sticks Together!

By now, you understand and realize the life-enhancing benefits of martial arts for your children aged 3-5, 6-11, and teenagers.

But do you also understand and realize that the life-enhancing benefits of martial arts are not just for children, but for you too? And herein lies the twist ending of the 9 secrets. What about you?

Have you ever considered stepping across the mat, donning a uniform, and training in martial arts alongside your children? The number one demographic at my family-oriented academy is parents in their 30s-40s training alongside their school-aged children. Does this describe you?

Yes, it's true, we all want the best for our children. But don't our children need the best of us?

Imagine if you could benefit from the physical benefits of martial arts training: stress release, calorie burning, weight loss, greater stamina, a boost in energy, learning to defend yourself and your family, if necessary, and having the health and fitness to be there for your children and grandchildren for years to come.

Imagine if you could benefit from the mental benefits of martial arts training: improved focus, greater clarity, enhanced self-discipline, a sharper mind to solve problems, and total confidence to achieve your own personal goals and career aspirations.

Imagine if you could benefit from the spiritual benefits of martial arts training: deciding to keep your work life from destroying your family life, living your life to the fullest, enjoying the prime years of your children's growth and development with them instead of watching from the sidelines, feeling the immense sense of pride and fulfillment of not just doing something for your children, but doing something with them, creating memories that you will cherish for a lifetime.

The greatest gift you can give as a parent to help your children achieve success is not gift certificates, toys, or video games. The greatest (and hardest) gift you can give is the gift of your time and of yourself. Children don't want our presents; more than anything, they want our presence. It's not so much what we do for our children, it's what we do with our children that matters most.

So I invite you to join forces with your children and to participate in a family martial arts training program – together. You will be ever so grateful that you did and your children will carry their experience with you in their hearts forever.

Student Success Stories

I'm proud that my four children look up to me as a fellow student of Taekwon-Do, and understand that this is a life-long activity. – Deanne D., age 44

I love the stress relief during weeks when I have to make difficult business decisions. I've improved my physical conditioning and health. And I get a peaceful night's sleep after training in the martial arts, which for me is the best way to start another challenging day with energy, motivation and confidence. – Julio P., age 50

It is not sufficient to achieve fitness, like a solitary mountain peak – fitness is something you achieve and maintain, like rolling hills. – Dominic G., age 45

I have benefited from my martial arts training through effective stress management and conflict resolution. When we are stressed, we often lose the ability to see clearly and look beyond that stressful instance. Martial arts training offers a moment of reflection so that you can view your stress from outside. When we need to resolve conflict, we require a certain level of wisdom which martial arts fosters by strengthening values such as dignity, humility, deference, and self- esteem. – Kamel D., age 50

I have learned that everybody needs a balance in life. It is important to take time for yourself, get some exercise and get away from "things" for awhile. At the proverbial end of the road, not many people have ever said, "Wow, the years have flown by so quickly ... I wish I had spent more time at the

*office." After eight years and counting, I am happy
to be able to say "Wow, the years have gone by
quickly ... I'm glad I started Taekwon-Do with my
kids when I did"!* – Bob J., age 51

9 Success Tips

As you prepare to embark on the journey of Black Belt Excellence and family martial arts training, here are 9 success tips:

1. Clear your mind and your schedule and plan to train at least twice per week.

2. Be brave. The hardest push-up is not the last one, it's the first one.

3. Keep an open mind and an open heart to the wonderful journey that awaits.

4. For kids, I always say, "Push yourself!" For parents, I always say, "Pace yourself!"

5. Accept your limitations and inform your instructor accordingly.

6. Lead by example. If you're tired from work and you don't feel like going to class, then you're teaching your kids that any excuse can stop you from achieving your goals. If you go to train anyway, you're teaching perseverance.

7. Motivation follows action. Getting out of the house is always the hardest thing to do. But

once you take action and get your family to the dojo, your motivation will surely follow.

8. You must remain steadfast on your journey to greatness.

9. Be willing to wear the white belt. Be ready to take on a new challenge alongside your family members.

Student Success Story

I learned the importance of being a good role model. Many times I dragged myself to Taekwon-Do class late on a cold winter's night and asked myself, "Why I am I still doing this ... I'm exhausted!" But if I'm not motivated, the children are not motivated and so I have to push myself. My sons are always watching! – Kirsten J.

The Challenge – Are You Willing to Wear the White Belt?

To be the best parent you can be, for your children to be the best they can be, for your family to be the best it can be, here's a question for you: Are you willing to wear the white belt?

Are you willing to try something new, challenging, and yet extremely rewarding?

Are you prepared to put yourself in a vulnerable position where you are not an authority or an expert on a subject and be a beginner, just like your children?

Are you willing to go barefooted and embark on a humbling and yet empowering journey with your children?

Are you willing to wear the white belt, set goals for yourselves as a family, and overcome obstacles to achieve them so you can feel the exhilaration of achieving Black Belt, which is a metaphor for personal excellence?

If so, then start your search for a good family martial arts training program through the Internet.

You can also refer to my free .pdf, *Parents' Guide to Choosing a Great Family Martial Arts Training School* found here: www.blackbeltexcellencebook.com

May a great family martial arts training program help you live the family life of your dreams on your journey to Black Belt Excellence!

Student Success Story

It's funny how a series of circumstances leads life's path. As a family of four, we began our martial arts training at different times, beginning when my younger son Steven got an invitation for a Taekwon-Do Back-to-School demonstration from his friend whose dad was taking classes.

Based on our observations of how classes were conducted, the positive atmosphere and the encouragement given by the instructors, we figured that this may be a way for our kids to protect

themselves against potential bullies and as a means to get some physical exercise.

We figured we could join in with them, and then when they were comfortable enough to be left on their own, be on our way.

Well, fast forward fourteen years later. We are still training together as a family, though my older son has moved on and is living on his own. What we have come to realize is that there are few physical activities or opportunities where we can do something constructive together as a family.

Through martial arts training we have gained a multitude of skills, learned how to defend ourselves and have developed much more self-confidence by participating in tournaments and by teaching classes. We are able to keep fit and challenge ourselves even though we each have varying physical capabilities. My son has done extremely well in primary and secondary school and through university, particularly in demonstrating his self-confidence in speaking in front of others.

We never dreamed of achieving what we have, but now we are so happy to continue our journey together as a family as we help other families grow and develop, learn to focus, and take a path toward success in their lives. It's especially rewarding to see other families train together as we have, as we know exactly how they feel. We have also met a lot of amazing people along the way.

In the beginning, we saw martial arts as a means for our children to deal with potential bullying situations, get physical exercise and later, as a way to do something together as a family. Now, we continue working together, teaching and passing along our experience and expertise to others. It is an epic and continuing journey which we are fortunate to be taking together. - Wayne and Nelly D.

Acknowledgements

Thank you to my own family for inspiring me on the journey of Black Belt Excellence.

My mother Thérèse Trân Nguyen for her love and sacrifices.

My father Nguyen Thanh Lam (1944-2008) for getting me and my brothers started in Taekwon-Do.

My martial arts family of past and present instructors, Leadership Team members, and students for their loyalty, support, and dedication.

My wife Amelia Nguyen and my sons Justice and Jackson who inspire me every day.

Top 9 Reasons to Buy This Book Now!

1. When people ask you, you will be able to answer, "Yes, I am a ninja."

2. Chuck Norris says so.

3. The family that kicks together, sticks together!

4. "There is no charge for awesomeness, or attractiveness." – Kung Fu Panda

5. You can build your character, one kick at a time.

6. You will learn why family martial arts training is not about violence, it's about virtues.

7. Martial arts played a major role in a #1 *New York Times* Best Seller's life. *"Martial arts was HUGE in my life. It is one of the BEST things that ever happened to me. Martial arts also taught me about respect, physical and mental mastery, and the overarching virtue of commitment and discipline in a positive way at an early age. I think more people should do martial arts."* – Brendon Burchard, #1 *New York Times* Best Seller of *The Millionaire*

Messenger and *The Charge – Activating the
10 Human Drives That Make You Feel Alive*

8. You will read real-life Student Success
   Stories of children, teenagers, parents, and
   families who are just like you whose lives
   were transformed through family martial arts
   training.

9. The journey of a thousand miles begins with
   one step. This book helps you take that first
   step towards living the life of your dreams
   through family martial arts training.

About Master Phil Nguyen (and Photo)

Hello. My name is Master Phil, author of *Black Belt Leadership – 9-Point Path to Wisdom, Inspiration, and Enlightenment.*

I'm a 7th Degree Black Belt in Taekwon-Do, a 1st Degree Black Belt in Jiu-Jitsu, and a White Belt in Parenting (and always will be because my 2 ninja sons teach me something new every day).

I am a martial artist first, a #1 best-selling author/speaker/mind-body-spirit teacher second, and an entrepreneur third.

Ultimately, all of my work is about helping people like you gain more happiness in your heart, health in your body, and honor in your soul through martial arts training, wisdom, and philosophy (because nurturing your 3 treasures of mind, body, and spirit, which is what martial arts is all about, is a beautiful thing).

I bow to your awesomeness.

For information on my Black Belt Leadership Programs visit: www.BlackBeltLeadership.com.

www.ingramcontent.com/pod-product-compliance
Lightning Source LLC
Chambersburg PA
CBHW041357090426
42739CB00001B/1